Effective Baby and Toddler Discipline

7 Steps to Transform Explosive Child and Eliminate Tantrums. For Children Ages 1- 5

Table Of Contents

Introduction

Disciplining a toddler is both a vital and delicate act. It is a balancing act that parents need to really talk and decide about because this will make or break the formation of the child. Before the onset of globalization and the spread of online information, the act of disciplining solely depended on cultural, the religious, and racial background. Some cultures believe in corporal punishment even in young children. The Christian biblical verse "He who withholds his rod hates his son, But he who loves him disciplines him diligently" is taken as a provident sign that physical consequence is necessary to show love and to protect the child. On the other hand, other cultures believe in maximum tolerance when disciplining young children. Now that disciplining methods have become more scientific with the psychological basis, parents are now being taught and rewired into disciplining according to the internal needs of the child.

Chapter 1: The Anatomy of a Tantrum

Before this book goes into detail on how to transform explosive toddlers into calm children, it may be helpful for parents to know what tantrums really are, its causes, and its symptoms. Your full understanding of what tantrums are will help you distinguish a regular bad-hair-day episode from a full-blown emotional tantrum.

What is a Tantrum?

A tantrum is a physical and emotional period that displays intense emotions such as anger, frustration, and discomfort. An emotional tantrum is usually portrayed through shouting, screaming, intense crying, stomping, grabbing and throwing objects, and lying stiffly on the floor.

Tantrums usually occur in very young children from 15 months to 4 years of age. It is a normal occurrence and, in fact, considered as part of the developmental milestone that engages toddlers in handling different life situations. Tantrums are used as a means to communicate since toddlers this age still have difficulty with verbal expression. As it is used a means to communicate, every child that throws an emotional tantrum needs an audience. A tantrum can last as short as 30 seconds and as long as 5 minutes.

What Causes Tantrums?

Tantrums may be triggered by all sorts of events. It can be sparked by something adults will consider as very shallow or much unexpected.

Lack of Attention

One of the most common reasons why toddlers throw tantrums is the feeling of being neglected. Even if the parents do shower their toddlers with much attention, the moment that attention dissipates even for a while, that moment can turn into a feeling of being left alone and may lead to a tantrum episode. And since the toddler feels neglected, he/she will throw a show usually in public places to immediately catch, not only the parents' attention but also the entire population around him/her.

Extreme Irritation

Irritation or frustration is another major cause of tantrums. As mentioned above, toddlers have difficulty expressing themselves verbally. This inability causes irritability especially when toddlers are trying to express something but their parents cannot fully grasp what it is. This commonly occurs in toddlers aged 2 to 4 years old. Once they develop their communication skills, such emotional outbursts should slowly fade away.

Extreme Hunger or Thirst

Adults do also throw fits when they are hungry or thirsty, what more toddlers. Extreme hunger or thirst do trigger old infants or young toddlers to throw fits especially if their parents have not responded immediately to their basic needs.

Failure to Get What They Want

For older toddlers who are starting to develop their inner will and decision-making skills, not getting what they want will definitely trigger tantrums.

Exhaustion

When infants or toddlers are overstimulated and they are extremely tired, it causes feelings of irritation and frustration too and the only way they can communicate that they are tired is by throwing a tantrum.

What are the Symptoms of a Tantrum?

It is also important for parents to know whether a tantrum is brewing to nip it in the bud. Early detection is truly the best remedy for any situation. With your watchful eyes, do see whether your child is about to throw one to know whether you should act on it or ignore it.

Defiance and Deviance

Your toddler is about to throw a tantrum soon once you see oppositional behaviour that lasts for more than 15 minutes. Whether it is the refusal to wear shoes or the sudden deviation from your common family routine, your toddler might be on the brink of a tantrum episode.

Sudden Silence

If you notice your toddler's mood change abruptly from bubbly to complete silence, then something must have happened. This symptom usually happens when your toddler is interrupted while playing with his/her toys or with other toddlers. When this happens, look at the body language of your toddler. Check if he/she is staring at something or someone strangely or if he/she is pouting.

Heavy Breathing

When your toddler is upset or frustrated at something or someone, his/her breathing pattern usually shifts from normal respiration to heavy breathing. Heavy breathing could be a reaction to the feeling of anger and it is only a matter seconds or minutes until your toddler screams or cries out loud.

What kind of Tantrums raise Red Flags?

As mentioned above, tantrums are normal occurrences for young children from 1 year to 5 years old. It is part of every child's development process and every parent must prepare to contain their children every so often. It is still normal for toddlers to throw tantrums once in a while but tantrums that occur daily or regularly may pose some behavioural or even developmental issues that need to be addressed. Tantrum frequency, as well as the frequency of untoward behaviours exhibited during each tantrum episode, may be conclusive that a child has neurological or mental health needs. Determining the red flags early on is best for the child's sake and for the parents' peace of mind.

1. **Violence and Hostility**

   It was mentioned in the earlier parts of the book that toddlers throw tantrums due to extreme anger or frustration so it may be normal for them to act a little violent or hostile towards their caregivers or towards their environment. However, if there is the consistent display of hostility with a mix of aggression in last 20 to 30 tantrum episodes then that should raise a red flag. It is not a normal sight to see a toddler hurt his/her parents because of not getting what he/she wants but if this becomes a regular occurrence, then it best to consult a Developmental Pediatrician.

2. Lingering Episodes of Tantrums

Tantrums normally last 5 to 10 minutes but if a toddler's tantrum fits consistently linger longer than 20 minutes then it should raise a red flag. Lingering episodes of tantrums simply mean the child has minimal ability to compose oneself, unlike other toddlers. If this happens all the time, parents are suggested to note down their toddler's behaviours during each episode so that they can discuss this in full detail with their child's doctor.

3. Self-Inflicted Injuries

If it is not normal for toddlers to hurt their parents, it is all the more not normal for toddlers to hurt themselves out of frustration or anger. Banging one's head on the wall or floor, scratching or biting one's skin until it bleeds, or using toys or any object in the environment to hit oneself definitely raises the red flag. Toddlers that do this with frequency and consistency must immediately be brought to the doctor for further observation.

Some of these red flag indications may be observed with normal toddlers so as parents you need to be observant to see whether your toddler's behaviour during a tantrum fit is still within normal bounds. Just remember that frequency and consistency are both red flag indications; so if your toddler bit you once but didn't do it again then that is normal. However, if your toddler kicks you consistently every day, then that could be an indication of a behavioural issue.

Now that the causes, symptoms, and even the red flags of tantrums have been discussed, it is now time to give you the step by step process on how to transform your explosive toddler into a calm, behaved angel.

Chapter 2: Step 1 – Know Your Child's Current State

Parents cannot arrest every toddler's tantrum episode if they do not know the current psychological and behavioural characteristics of a child aged 1 to 5 years old. There are many scientific and medical studies that show and prove that tantrums normally occur to children within this age range. Because of the plentiful evidence, there must be something within the psychological and physiological wiring of every toddler that will lead him/her to throw tantrums. In order to understand what every child aged 1 to 5 years old go through, here are their universal physical, psychological, behavioural, and emotional development milestones:

Physical Development Milestones

At the onset of your child's first birthday, he/she is already exiting the infancy stage and is moving towards the toddler stage. One of the signs that prove this transition period is learning to walk. Once your child starts walking independently between 15 months to 18 months, get ready for the drastic changes that will happen to you, as a parent, and to your child, as a toddler. Walking independently sparks an internal switch in your child's being. It is the feeling of self-reliance, self-confidence, self-control, and overall self-esteem that is being developed as your child learns to walk. Because of these external and internal changes, you will notice a great change in your child's demeanor. From the total dependence during the infancy stage, you will notice refusal to hold your hand while striding and this will somehow give you separation anxiety.

Aside from learning to walk, at this stage, your child's body will appear more proportion than when he/she was an infant. From ages 1 to 2 years, your child's arms, legs, and torso will elongate and this will increase his height to about 86 cm and 85 cm for male and female toddlers respectively. Because of the increase in height, your child's weight will also increase drastically to about 11kg. As your child reaches 2 years of age, his/her physical development will slow down until his/her 3rd birth year. After the third year, your child will go through another drastic physical growth until the 5th year.

Psychological Development Milestones

According to the famous Italian Educator and Psychologist, Maria Montessori, children aged 0 to 6 years are undergoing what she called the First Plane of Development. Children within the First Plane of Development undergo a multitude of physical and psychological changes as this is essential in the formation of the person your child will be in the future. This is the most crucial development stage in your child's life and it is, therefore, essential for parents, like you, to know what to expect and what to do during these crucial years.

During this crucial phase, your child's entire being can be compared to a camera. Your child constantly takes mental pictures of anything and everything he/she sees, hears, feels, tastes, and touches. As his/her brain takes all these information in, he/she tries to mimic these mental notes through his words and deeds. For sure you have heard your child parrot your own words and even your actions. That is how receptive your child is during this stage, so as parents you need to be careful of your words and deeds in front of your child.

The First Plane of Development concentrates on the formation of the future adult within the child so it is only rational that this phase makes the child egocentric. Psychologist Sigmund Freud also affirms that both the Ego and the Superego are developed from 0 to 6 years of age. You might be wondering what egocentricity is and how it is manifested by your child. Egocentricity means having no regard for others except oneself. This is totally not a bad attitude for children between 1 to 5 years old. The entire being of the child needs to undergo a series of developments, for this reason, the child must concentrate on himself first. This is the stage when you will often hear your child say "mine" and will claim ownership of anything and everything at home as well as often hear the word "no" to reject everything and anything you are offering. Do not take this against your child. Claiming ownership of everything does not necessarily mean that your child is selfish; likewise saying "no" to everything does not necessarily mean that your child is hard-headed. Doing these is a means to understand the environment around him. This is the perfect time to instil good manners and right conduct to your child. Gently explain using words that are understandable to him/her the difference between right and wrong. Mind you, you need to repeat all these explanations over and over again.

In connection to being egocentric, your child at this stage will be very satisfied playing by himself/herself. It is also a natural instinct for your child to be happily playing or working alone because of the natural need to develop oneself. Even if you bring him/her to the park or to the nearby public sandbox, you will see your child dig alone. If your child is almost 5 or 5 years old, that age is the more social age so it becomes more natural to play with other kids; otherwise be happy to see your child happy alone. It is not because he doesn't have any social skills but because of his egocentric being.

Finally, your child at this stage is a tactile learner. He/She loves to use his/her hands to touch everything that he/she sees. Unless the object that he/she wishes to touch poses the danger, let your child hold whatever he/she wishes. This stage is the time to develop the 5 senses and touching is one of them. It is through the sense of touch that the child learns about the environment. It is also through manipulation of objects that your child's brain develops; therefore preventing your child to manipulate and touch equates to hindering your child's brain development.

Behavioural and Emotional Development Milestones

The emotional and behavioural state of your child at this stage is somewhat yin and yang. Children between 1 to 5 years old want independence yet are still clinging on to their parents. Children at this stage need to be assured and reassured of parental love, attention, and security so that they can venture out on their own. Parents must be able to provide such emotional support otherwise the child will be unsettled most of the time. It is best for parents to develop the sense of freedom within limits to their toddlers because it is at this stage when toddlers do test their parents' limits as well as their own limitations. Again, be consistent when defining the limitations so that your toddler will remember those set limitations eventually.

Children at this stage also demand order and familiarity. You have probably noticed your 2 to 5-year-olds voluntarily fixing their toys, picking up trash, or even wiping the table. It is because physical and environmental order are what your child needs so that he/she will also have internal order. If your house is untidy, this feeds bad images to your child; thus will have affected his overall mood and may even trigger a tantrum. It is best to involve your child in maintaining order in the home by demonstrating where to put his/her toys, where to put dirty dishes, where to put his/her clothes and shoes, and the like.

It is important for parents to satisfy the internal needs of the child because that is the way to prevent tantrums. Knowing your child's current physical and psychological needs are vital in determining how to control your child's emotions. Parents must be aware of all these so that their toddlers will have a happy, orderly environment.

Chapter 3: Step 2 – Create an Orderly Environment

As mentioned at the last part of the previous chapter, an orderly environment promotes internal order within the child. Parents need not wait for their child to burst out with extreme emotions before they feel the need to transform their homes into a tidy haven. You need not have your house undergo the extreme makeover; you just need to set up your house into a child-friendly one.

There are several ways and steps to achieve a fully orderly environment for your toddler. It does not only require having a clean house but also requires the entire family's full commitment to sustain it.

1. **Put child-sized furniture in the house**

   Remember that your child wants to have a sense of independence yet at the same time still have that sense of parental security as their safety net. One way to provide a means of independence within the home is making common household activities and chores accessible and doable for your toddlers.

   The easiest room to transform is your toddler's bedroom. Start with his/her bed. Choose a bed that is child-size so that he/she can easily climb on and off the bed without your help. Having a bed that not too overwhelming for your toddler will avoid pre and post-sleep tantrums. Aside from a child-size bed, you can also add a set of child-size chair and desk where your child can draw, write, paint, and play. Giving your toddler his/her own desk and chair will feed his ego and sense of ownership and will allow him to be more confident when working alone. Lastly, it would also be nice if your toddler can have a bathroom that has child-size/child-height fixtures. Having a basin installed to your toddler's height will teach him hygiene early on without being dependent on you. Imagine your child happily washing his hands, brushing his teeth, and washing his face without having the fear of falling off a chair or a stepper.

2. Color-Coordinate his/her things

Another way of creating order in the home is color-coordinating your toddler's things. Your toddler cannot yet read but he/she can definitely recognize colors. To easily remind your child where to put things, color-coordination is the best solution. For example, all his yellow-colored toys should go in the yellow-colored bin. All his used white clothes should go in the white bin. All the blue-colored books go in the blue cubby hole.

If you cannot color-coordinate the entire house because it's quite tedious and costly, at least color-coordinate your toddler's room. For the first month, demonstrate to your child where to put particular stuff and for sure your child will pick this up without any problem. Your child is quite a neat-freak at this age and you will be surprised by how much orderly he/she can be with just a few demonstrations.

3. Have a designated place for everything

Apart from putting child-size furniture or fixtures and color-coordinating your toddler's things, another way to create order in the home is assigning a designated place for everything. Similar to color-coordinating, you must train your toddler where to put back things that your toddler will use. Teaching through demonstration will help your child remember where to put specific objects.

Start in your child's bedroom. It is best to have open cabinets or cubby holes so it will be easier for your child to put back his things. Assign a specific cabinet space or cubby hole for his/her shoes, his/her books, his/her bags, and much more. Repetition and consistency is the key in instilling in your child order in his/her room. If he/she happens to misplace his stuff, just gently call his/her attention and show your toddler the correct place for his stuff.

When your child is already used to the idea, bring this practice outside his bedroom. Have designated areas for your remote controls, for your throw pillows, and other home items. To maintain such order and consistency, all the members of the family must commit to the same order and consistency. You must educate your partner as well as your other children that order is needed to avoid any potential emotional outbursts in your toddler so they need to be committed to this new system.

4. Involve your toddler in house chores

Another way to encourage your toddler's need for independence and self-reliance is by involving him/her in doing household chores. Aside from making him feel like one of the grown-ups in the house and making him feel independent, you are also exhausting his/her extra energy which can prevent possible tantrum episodes.

Since your toddler is with you all the time, demonstrate to him/her how to set up the dining table. Assign to him/her menial tasks like laying down the place mats to setting up the table if your child is older. You can also assign him/her to help you separate the whites from the colored clothes before doing the laundry. You can also ask your child to help you bring out the trash or help you walk the dog.

All of these tasks may be simple to your older children or to you but these tasks will be taken real seriously by your toddler. So when you do assign such tasks, talk to your toddler with all seriousness so he/she will feel that he/she is sharing the house responsibilities and is really part of the entire family. It is never too young for your toddler to take part in normal house activities. The earlier you involve your child, the more he/she will develop physically and emotionally.

5. Make sure the entire family adheres to the new home system

Since repetition and consistency are the most important ingredient in making this new home system successful, you need to make sure that your entire family is on the same page with you and all agree to follow the new system. All of you are looked up to and idolized by your toddler so if he/she sees that everyone in the house does the exact same thing and follow the exact same rule, he/she will not feel left out or ostracized. One way to convince your family to follow the new system is to explain to them that such changes are being done in order to prevent any temper tantrums in the future.

Chapter 4: Step 3 – Set Clear Rules

You go to the park with your toddler for a morning stroll and playtime. You sit on the bench while you observe your child play at the sandbox by the big slide. Your child enjoys filling his tiny bucket with sand using his tiny trowel. After 30 minutes, you decide it is time to go home to prepare the family's weekend lunch. You call your toddler and ask him to get ready to go. He says a firm "NO" and so you pick him up from the sandbox. He starts kicking the air and shouts "NO" while you try to buckle him in his stroller. Your son makes a scene at the park and you feel helpless. Is this a typical scene? Or is there something wrong here?

Both answers to these questions are yes. Yes, toddlers have huge tendencies to throw temper tantrums from time to time. So answer the question "Is this a typical scene?" is a definite yes; however, there is something wrong in the situation which caused the toddler to create a scene. Toddlers throw tantrums for a variety of reasons: they have difficulty expressing themselves, they have been interrupted without prior notice, they are hungry, they are tired, they are frustrated and much more. So what sparked the tantrum of the toddler in the example? He threw a tantrum because he was interrupted without prior notice.

This is just one of the many possible situations that may cause a toddler to throw a temper tantrum. The next big question is "Is there a way to prevent it?" The answer to this question is dependent on the parent. Parents of toddlers must have the biggest amount of patience because tantrum prevention requires consistency, repetition, and firmness. Parents must also have the right amount of discipline to carry out the required level of consistency in front of their toddlers. If you have all of these qualities, then you will not have any difficulty preventing temper tantrums.

As discussed in the first step, the best way to prevent tantrums is to know the internal wiring of your toddler. One of the many complexities of the internal wiring of your child is the external and internal need for order. In the situation above, the toddler had been playing with sand for a good 30 minutes – filling and unloading his tiny bucket over and over again. As an adult, you think 30 minutes is long enough for your toddler to feel tired and bored with the exercise but that is not what is inside your child's brain. In your child's mind, he thinks he has not yet perfected the method of filling and unloading the bucket so he needs more time at the sandbox. This complete opposite mind frame will really spark a tantrum. So does a parent meet the mind of their toddler? One of the best ways is to communicate to them. Yes, toddlers have difficulty expressing themselves but they can totally understand their parents. And parents must constantly communicate to their toddlers to achieve the meeting of the minds.

To prevent situations such as the example above, parents must tell their toddlers of their schedule in a manner that is understandable to their toddlers. This commences the exercise of setting clear rules for the child to follow. For example, the mother of the toddler prior to leaving for the park should have talked to his son and said that they are going to the park for a short while so she can prepare food for the family. Telling the toddler once may not be enough so the mother should tell her toddler at least three times before setting out for the park. Also, prior to leaving the mother must have made sure that her toddler understood her. One way of knowing whether she was understood was by looking at the toddler at eye level and getting a nod. At the park, the mother should have observed that her toddler, as focused as he is, had lost the sense of time. Instead of just telling her son they had to go that very moment, she should have given her son timestamps like "We need to go in 5 minutes buddy, okay? Remember, Mommy needs to make lunch for Daddy, Mommy, and you." Then after a few minutes, give another time stamp. Finally, the mother should have given him a minute to get ready to go before leaving the place. This way, the toddler is conditioned to leave in a short while and he understands why he needs to leave the sandbox.

Of course, the first attempt or even the second attempt to set clear rules for your toddler to follow may not be as successful as depicted in the example. Nevertheless, do not get discouraged right away. Try and try and try over and over again until such time that your toddler gets used to the exercise of following instructions and learns to follow schedules.

Here are some reminders on how to set clear rules with your toddler:

1. Speak your Toddler's Language

You are not being asked to "baby talk" your toddler. That is actually the worst thing to do. What "speak your toddler's language" means to use basic, ordinary, daily words when speaking to your toddler. You have to remember that your toddler is still enriching his word bank so he/she may not understand terms such as office, laundry, vehicle, or schedule. Instead of using such terms say work, wash clothes, car, or time to make more understandable for your toddler.

2. Follow a Routine

As part of your toddler's inner need for order, it will be easier for you and your child to just follow a specific routine every single day. If you schedule morning strolls and playtime every weekend, make sure you follow exact time and duration. Even if your toddler cannot read time, his internal body clock will automatically alert his brain that it's time for a stroll or it's time to go home. If daily or weekly activities become second nature to your toddler, he/she will not see any reason to throw a tantrum.

3. Be Consistent

For sure you feel bombarded by this reminder already but, truth be told, consistency is really the only way to prevent temper tantrums. You need to consistent to your toddler especially when it comes to following a routine, disciplining him/her, praising him/her, and caring for him/her. You also need to be consistent with your other children and even your spouse. If you are only consistent with your toddler but very lenient with the other members of your family, your toddler can detect your contradictions and can get confused with your rules.

It is never too early for your toddler to follow certain rules and certain schedules. It is naturally easy for children their age to follow such routines because of their need for order. It is actually an inborn trait that toddlers have inherited since their infancy days, so parents must just naturally follow that trend to create peace within the child.

Chapter 5: Step 4 - Arrest Tantrum Triggers

As a parent, it is always better to be two steps ahead rather than be stuck in a sticky situation which could have been avoided. This also is true when it comes to preventing temper tantrums with your toddlers. As previously discussed in Chapter 2, temper tantrums are caused by a variety of triggers and situations some of which are hunger, fatigue, frustration, and anger. All of these triggers cause some of the worst tantrum episodes which parents regret not paying attention to instead of nipping the symptoms at the bud. Before you tire yourself out of calming your explosive child, this chapter will give detailed situations and specific solutions to common tantrum triggers.

"I am Sleepy"

Sophia picked up her daughter, Alice, from Day Care this morning. Sophia usually drives straight home while Alice snoozes in the back seat. Sophia does this routine every day except today. Sophia has to rush to the grocery because she forgot to buy milk the other day. As soon as she buckled Alice in the car seat, she informed her daughter that they will quickly pass by the grocery before going home. Since Alice did not make a fuss in the car going to the grocery, Sophia thought Alice can spare a few more minutes in the grocery and decides grab bread, cereals, and diapers. While picking bread, Alice suddenly grabbed a couple of bags of bagels and didn't want to let it go. Sophia tried to play tug-O-war to get the bagel but Alice just won't let it go. As soon as the tug-O-war ended, Alice cried her heart out.

Can you point out Alice's tantrum trigger? Alice's tantrum trigger was actually her mother, Sophia. Her mother knew Alice's daily routine. She always slept in the car after Day Care and slept more at home.

What would you have done if you were Sophia? You should have followed Alice's routine. Knowing that your toddler sleeps at a certain time should be an indication that you need to leave that schedule free from any errands. Adults should work their schedules around the routines of their children, most especially when it is napping time. Breaking your child's nap time is equal to depriving him/her of a meal or a play time. This will definitely cause a tantrum because your child cannot explain the woozy feeling inside him/her.

"I am Hungry"

Felicia, a mother of two boys, normally brings her toddler Julian with her every time she picks up her eldest son every afternoon. The time she normally leaves the house is about 30 minutes before the afternoon snack schedule of Julian. Since the travel time to her son's school and back to their house is around 20 minutes, Felicia does not bother to bring crackers or milk in the car. Unfortunately, that afternoon, a multiple vehicle mishaps occupied the entire road and they had to take a long detour to get home. The regular 20 minutes travel time extended to an hour and Julian was growing hungrier by the minute. In the car, he started pulling the hair of his older brother which caused two tantrum episodes at the same time.

What was Julian's tantrum trigger? Julian's temper tantrum was triggered by extreme hunger. Even if he did not express it through crying, the fact that he acted frustrated and hostile to his older brother proved that he was indeed feeling hungry. Parents must understand that the feeling of hunger sometimes does not translate to toddlers the same way it translates to adults. For toddlers, the feeling of hunger equates to anger or frustration because they still cannot tell emotions and sensations apart.

What would you have done if you were Felicia? Parents must always be two steps ahead when it comes to their children. Every time you leave your house, regardless whether your child's meal time is still a few hours after your travel time, you must always bring the essentials such as extra clothes, diapers, snacks, milk, and water. Similar to the case above, Felicia assumed that they will be home in a jiffy but due to unforeseen events they arrived home later than Felicia thought. Julian's feeling of hunger led to uneasiness which led him to direct his attention to the older brother. This would have been prevented had Felicia been two steps ahead and prepared snacks for both kids. Giving food to her kids would have redirected their attention to their meals.

"I Need Space"

First-time parents, Bill and Stephanie, are excited to bond with their toddler Zack every afternoon after work. One particular afternoon, Bill surprised Zack with a bag full of building blocks. Zack got the bag with a big smile on his face and Bill got so excited that he decided to play with Zack's building blocks as well. Bill followed Zack to his room and poured the contents of the bag on the floor. Bill demonstrated to Zack how to use the building blocks but Zack knocked down every single structure that his father made. Bill stopped his son from knocking down the blocks and forced Zack to build something similar to his. Instead of following Bill, Zack started throwing the blocks all the room and started shouting "No." Bill scolded Zack for his bad behaviour and even threatened to not give any more toys to Zack. This even added Zack's emotional outburst. The commotion forced Stephanie to step out of the kitchen and step in between the father and son.

What was Zack's tantrum trigger? Unfortunately, Zack's tantrum trigger is his father, Bill. Bill was more excited to play with the building blocks he bought for Zack that he invaded Zack's playing time and space. Parents must understand that toddler require individual play time because they have an internal need for independence. Zack must have been given time and space to manipulate the building blocks on his own and find his own way of stacking up the blocks. However, the eagerness of Bill to teach Zack was viewed by Zack as overbearingness and elicited a negative reaction from Zack. The negative reaction of Zack was viewed by Bill by disrespect which led Bill to say threatening words to Zack. The snowball effect of a simple issue resulted to a temper tantrum.

What would you have done if you were Bill? Parents must give enough space for their toddlers to observe. Space means leaving them to manipulate objects on their own yet still being physically there to observe them and to make sure they are safe. Parents sometimes assume that their toddlers are helpless and totally ignorant beings but what they do not know is that their toddlers are very much capable of handling themselves within a child-friendly environment. If you were Bill, just hand out the toy, demonstrate how it is properly used once, and let your child freely play with it. Longing to play with your child after a long day at work is natural but your toddler is not yet ready to play with another individual so you need to respect your toddler's space.

Chapter 6: Step 5 - Introduce New Activities

Boredom is one of the triggers of temper tantrums. Toddlers, especially those who have not reached the preschool age, normally stay in the house longer than most of their siblings or parents. If the home is the regular play area of toddlers, there will come a day when toddlers have explored every part of the house and are out of new discoveries to keep them busy. When this happens, parents or caregivers will notice the toddlers become more disruptive and short-tempered. To avoid this from happening, parents and caregivers must always be ready with new and exciting activities to keep their toddlers busy and interested. This chapter will give extensive suggestions for both indoor and outdoor activities fit for toddlers.

Before you overindulge on your toddler's new activities, be reminded that all the new activities you will introduce to your child must be part of his/her daily routine. Following a daily schedule keeps your toddler in proper order so new activities must coincide with the existing routine familiar to your child. If activity time is not yet part of your toddler's daily routine, slowly introduce this into his schedule every day. Do not suddenly allot an hour to do something new because for sure this can trigger a tantrum. Instead, introduce it 5 to 10 minutes per day until such time your child is used to the new activity. If you are going to introduce another activity after a couple of weeks, make sure to use the same time to not ruin the routine.

Appropriate Indoor Activities for Toddlers

1. Water Color Painting

Once your toddler reaches 24 to 30 months old, he/she starts recognizing and appreciating colors. It is, therefore, fitting for toddlers to be exposed to painting activities. The materials needed for painting are actually cheap and readily available in stores so it will not be difficult for parents to set up a small corner or outdoor area for painting.

Before you leave your child to paint on his/her own, make sure to establish clear rules. First, demonstrate how to properly handle the materials. Second, show your child where to hang his/her finished painting. Lastly, show your child how to clean up after. Take note all these demonstrations are just done through modelling. You do not even need to speak a single word. Just show your child how it is done. You will be surprised how well your toddler can follow directions to the smallest details.

Here are the materials that you will need:

- Easel board
- Paint brushes
- Water-based paints
- Waterproof aprons
- Clothesline
- Clothespin
- Cut out Manila papers

2. Playing Musical Instruments

Aside from the interest in colors, older toddlers are very sensitive to musical notes which make it the perfect time for them to be introduced to different musical instruments. Some instruments that are child-friendly are child-sized organs, tambourine, mini-guitars, and mini-drums.

Similar to how you introduced painting to your child, make sure you demonstrated well the proper usage and storage of the instruments. Show how to gently press the keys or to gently strum the strings, or to gently tap the tambourine to not create a loud noise. Keep everything orderly and manageable.

Once your child knows how to properly use the instruments and how to properly stow them away, let him/her play the music that he wants. Even if it sounds incoherent to you, for your child it is already a good melody. Prevent yourself from correcting your child except when he/she mishandles the material, instead give praises when he/she does the activity in an orderly fashion.

3. Cooking

Toddlers love to use their hands, especially in the kitchen. When you are doing easy dishes, you may involve your toddler and make him/her your assistant. You will be surprised how orderly and neat your toddler is.

Teach your child how to make pancakes or waffles. Your child will surely love to beat eggs, pour milk, mix the batter, and design the finished product. You can also teach your child how to prepare the salad for the family. Ask your child to peel of lettuce leaves and wash each leaf in the sink. You can also ask your child to help you set the table or clean up after meals.

Appropriate Outdoor Activities for Toddlers

Do not limit your child's activities inside the comforts of your house because your toddler definitely needs to go out and enjoy the environment as well. Introducing your child outdoors at an early age will not only help him/her get familiar with the elements outside your home but will also strengthen his physique.

1. **Outdoor Sports Activities**

   The worst thing that parents can do to their toddlers is to be afraid of them and to overprotect them. While it is normal for parents to be protective of their children, it is also deterring children to realize their full potentials. That is why it is important for parents to give spatial allowances between them and their children. It is okay for your kids to be hurt sometimes; they will learn a lot from those experiences.

   One outdoor sport that is appropriate for your toddlers is kickball, dodge ball, baseball, and the like. Since toddlers love to throw things, introduce them to a sport that satisfies that internal need to throw. Aside from satisfying an internal need to throw, these sports help improve your child's gross and fine motor skills plus hand-eye coordination and balance. You and your child can enjoy a few minutes playing ball. Just do not tire your child too much because this may cause tantrums in the evening.

2. Playground and Obstacle Games

Bringing your toddler to the playground is one way to take away his/her home boredom. Introduce your toddler to the various obstacle games present in the park or playground nearby. Always demonstrate how to perform such courses for safety. Let your toddler experience the tire game or the balance beam, but of course with your close supervision. Let your child experience other obstacle courses like crawling under arcs and the like. This will not only improve your child's physical strength, it will also improve his/her thinking skills as well as his/her patience and determination.

3. Outdoor Chores

Toddlers love to sweep. You will be surprised by how much patience and exactness they have in using the broom and the dustpan. If you have a huge lawn with dried leaves, bring your child out to the yard and demonstrate how to sweep the dried leaves. After a few demonstrations, give your child a child-sized broom and dustpan and you'll definitely enjoy your toddler go. Take pictures or videos of your child and show it to him/her when he/she is older.

The first five steps in transforming an explosive toddler into a calm one are long-term solutions as well as forward-thinking remedies to temper tantrums. These two steps do not actually wait for the toddler to throw a fit; instead, it helps prevent the frequency of tantrum episodes. Since these two steps are long-term solutions, its implementation requires time and consistency as well. With enough patience and love, both steps will reap rewards in the future and will help reveal a calmer toddler sooner than you think.

The remaining two steps to transforming an explosive toddler to a calm one are more short-term and will show immediate results. Even if it has short-term effects, all steps must still be carried out consistently so your toddler will know what to expect every time he/she throws a tantrum.

Chapter 7: Step 6–Show Composure

Imagine you are in the middle of finishing your grocery shopping or in the middle of attending church service when your toddler starts acting up and throws a tantrum in a public place, what would you do? How does one handle a toddler who wants to make a big scene in a public place? This must have happened to you more than once if you have a feisty toddler who wants you to finish your grocery shopping in a jiffy or wants to leave the church before the service ends. How did you handle such situation back then? Did you give in right away to your child? Or did you put your foot down and finished what you needed to finish before dealing with your child?

When your child starts acting up, do not panic nor lose your patience. If you shout at your child at the same time he/she is ranting, you are aggravating the situation. The unsettled child becomes more unsettled when he/she sees the all the more unsettled adult. Do not face fire with fire; instead be the water that will subside the flames. Remember that you are the adult and however way you will react will be copied by your child. Acting calmly will eventually influence your child to calmly face frustrations; while acting noisily will even reinforce the tantrum behaviour of your toddler.

Here are some tips in order to stay composed in the midst of an outburst:

1. **Count**

   Even before you start shouting at your raging toddler, close your eyes and start counting from 1 to 10 or even

100. Counting will give you ample time to regain your composure and will give you enough time to cool off.

2. Look elsewhere

If you are not yet ready to speak with your toddler, it is best to turn your attention to another person or object. Avoid eye contact because eye contact may either intensify the tantrum episode of your toddler or may tempt you to raise your voice at your child. Steer clear of your child first but make sure you do not leave him/her altogether. Remember, your child still needs to feel secure around you and you walking out may just add on to the tension and frustration that your child is feeling.

3. Move to a "safer" location

Once you have composed yourself, carry your child and move to a "safer" location. By "safer" location this means a place away from other people and away from objects that your child might pick up and throw. Since a toddler who throws a tantrum wants an audience, you need to remove him/her from the public eye and take him/her away from the audience. Select a corner with fewer distractions where you two can talk calmly.

4. See your toddler eye to eye

When you want to pacify your child in the middle of a tantrum episode, you need to bend down to your toddler's eye level and see him/her eye to eye. Speaking to your child eye to eye will give your child the impression that you are ready to listen to his/her needs at the same time you are showing that you are honest and serious.

5. Speak in a mild manner

Remember not to counter your toddler's tantrum episode with your own emotional fit. Charging your toddler angrily will not solve the problem. Shouting at your child to impose your authority will only work a couple of times and the rest of the time your child will just get used it. Instead of shouting at your child, try whispering to him/her. Your child will need to stop screaming and whining to hear you speak.

6. Distract your child

Attempting to reach a compromise with your toddler in the middle of a temper tantrum is synonymous to speaking to a wall. The best way to appease your frustrated child is by diverting his/her attention somewhere else. The younger your child is, the easier for you to distract him/her. If your toddler is throwing a fit indoor, bring him/her outdoor and divert his/her attention to the clouds or the sky or to something that would interest him/her.

7. Listen to music

Try singing your child's favourite nursery rhymes as a way of diverting your child's energy and changing your child's mood. Children love listening to catchy tunes especially toddlers aged 15 months to 4 years old. If you have access to the internet or you have an iPad handy, go to YouTube and search the compilation of nursery rhymes. For sure the music and the video will divert your child's attention. Encourage your child to sing with you.

There are many other ways to pacify your upset child but all these methods will not be effective if you will face your child without composure. Children are very intuitive and receptive to their parents' feelings. They immediately can detect if their parents are hesitant to speak with them or if their parents are very aggressive towards them. The kind of energy and emotion that you will project to your child will be projected back to you. Remember that your toddlers are like cameras that take mental pictures and mimic these mental pictures, so if you show hesitancy your child will project that too or if you show aggression your child will mirror that too.

Be patient and practice these methods with your child. See what will work and set back what will not. What is important is the way you deal with a frustrated toddler. Never use ill words nor use force. These will cause more tantrums in the future. Instead be a little more understanding and remind yourself that your child is just going through a phase which is part of his/her development. Be firm in carrying out the family rules at the same time be gentle in comforting and giving the needs of your child. It is indeed a real balancing act that every parent has to master.

Chapter 8: Step 7 – Stand your Ground or Step In

The biggest question parents ask when dealing with a toddler who is presently throwing a tantrum is "When do I step in?" This is a really difficult question to answer because there is no singular solution to handling an explosive toddler. Especially when you are in a public place, you immediately want to control the situation because you do not want to be a bother to other people. In order to give you a better view of the situation, this chapter will give some suggestions on when it is the right time to step in and the right time to stand your ground

Out in the Open

You are in a public place when your toddler suddenly throws a big one, do you stand your ground or step in? When you are in a public place, it is difficult to really handle a toddler throwing a fit. First, because there are a lot of unfamiliar people staring at you and your child. Second, because you are afraid that whatever you do reflects on how good or bad you are at parenting. Third, because you think people already concluded that you are the worst parent on earth. If these are what are on your mind while trying to handle the tantrum situation, then you will never solve the problem. The first thing you need to do is to erase all the negative thoughts in your head. It doesn't help you think wisely when you are pressuring yourself on preserving your parental image. Second, focus your attention on your explosive toddler and try to recall what you did earlier that could have caused the temper tantrum. Did you forget to feed him/her? Did he/she get enough naptime? Is he/she extremely tired? If one of the causes to the tantrums are one of these three questions, then arrest the situation by answering your child's basic. If the cause of the tantrum is not one of these three usual suspects, then stand your ground. Your child might be throwing a tantrum because he/she didn't get what he/she wants. If that is the case, remove your child from the public eye.

This situation called for you to analyze the possible trigger of your child's tantrum. If it is a basic need that he/she need, by all means, step in right away. A basic need is something that your child truly needs. However, if it is just a want that was not given that sparked the big emotional mess, then stand your ground. What you do not want to happen is to let your toddler get used to crying just to get what he/she wants. That is a manipulative move that toddlers tend to do and if parents immediately respond to this stimulus, the child will take it as a behaviour that elicits parental submission. That is the last thing that you want to happen. If you let this happen, get ready to be a slave to your child's desires.

Once you and your child are both calm, it is the time to talk to your child about what just happened. Explain to your child why he/she cannot get whatever it is that he/she wanted. Remind your child of the rules that you have set earlier. You can say "Remember, Mommy said we cannot stay too long in the park?" or "Remember, Mommy said we will go to the toy store to buy your cousin a birthday gift and you will help me pick one?" Reminders will help your child recall the previous agreements and will be able to connect the reason why his/her whims cannot be patronized at that moment. In closing, remind your child that you are not mad that he/she wanted to get to things but the behaviour that he/she did is something that is not nice. You may also add that his/her behaviour upset other children too or bothered other people. That way your child becomes more conscious of other people and becomes more aware of other people's feelings.

Great Big Fiasco

Ellen's toddler, Alicia, is at home solving the biggest puzzle of her life – buttoning her sweater. The entire family is about to eat out to celebrate a sibling's birthday. While everyone is ready to go, they all watch as Alicia takes long in buttoning her sweater. While waiting for Alicia, Ellen decides to go to the kitchen to ready the ingredients for tomorrow's breakfast. While she doing so, she heard Alicia scream her lungs out. She runs to the living area and sees Alicia on the floor stomping her feet and pounding her hands on the tiles. Alicia's sibling were all laughing as they watch Alicia's frustration grow bigger and bigger.

When a similar situation happens at home, the first thing that you should do is step in right away. Why? Because you need to stop your toddler from hurting himself/herself. Alicia's stomping and pounding may injure her so Ellen has to step in right away. The second thing you need to do is to instruct your other children to stop laughing at their younger sibling. Buttoning a sweater may be an easy task for an adult or an older child but for a toddler like Ellen, it is a great, big task that requires 100% focus. When her siblings laughed at her, it popped her frustration bubble and triggered a massive tantrum. The third thing that you need to do is bring your toddler to a room and talk calmly to him/her. Distract your toddler by saying nice things like "I saw you button your sweater. You were doing great sweetie!" Lastly, once your toddler is calm, talk to your other children and tell them not to poke fun at their younger sibling. You can also ask your spouse to settle the issue with the older kids while you handle the issue of your toddler.

As a parent, it is more difficult to stand ground than to step in. Parents are normally reactive individuals because of their unconditional love for their kids. So when kids do whine to get what they want, parents do give in because their hearts melt for their kids. The next time that happens, please do think of your child's future. Once your child is old enough, he/she will not know how to work hard for something because he/she just got it through his/her manipulation. Standing your ground is not the absence of love and care, it is actually showing love and care for your child's future.

Conclusion

Handling temper tantrums are just one of the many tasks or responsibilities of a parent. As a parent, you need to not just be physically and financially ready to raise a child but also mentally and spiritually prepared. Although there may be some rough roads ahead while rearing your child, there are many more smooth highways to look forward to. What you just need to do is to prepare for the long ride.

After reading this nook and after knowing what a tantrum is, what its causes and symptoms are, and what steps to take to arrest it, here are what parents need to remember:

1. **Know your child.**

   Knowing your child's internal development as well as interests and personality will prepare you for what's ahead. Remember that temper tantrums are a part of a toddler's inner coping mechanism so if he/she throws a fit once in a while do take it in stride. However, if he/she throws a tantrum more than what is expected, do assess whether you have gotten to know your child and have really answered his/her needs. Frequent tantrums may signal either a shortcoming on your end or a development issue which needs to be assessed by a Developmental Pediatrician.

2. **Know yourself.**

   You are now a parent. Your priorities must now be your family. So many changes have occurred in your life as of the moment. Before you spread yourself too thinly due to parental responsibilities, take some time alone and meditate. Get to know your current self. Relieve some stress by spending some alone time to either pray or do yoga. It is important for parents to press the reset button from time to time so they can be back on their feet stronger each time. Assessing yourself will prevent situations such as shouting at your child while throwing a fit or stressing out on your spouse.

3. Know your family.

If you have more than one child, there is a tendency to give more attention to the youngest member of the family than your older children; however, the truth of the matter is, everyone needs your attention. So remind yourself from time to time to spend time with every member of the family and make sure that you are still in tune with what is happening in their daily lives. You might be arresting a possible temper tantrum from your toddler but you have forgotten to prevent an emotional breakdown from your teenager. Do talk to all your children and of course your spouse every day. Touch base with all of them and let them know also how you feel.

Being a parent is a noble responsibility. It takes a lot of guts, patience, determination, and love to get through each day especially when raising a little one. Despite all your sacrifices, you know that you are doing a great job because you are raising your children the best way you can. For as long as you prioritize your children and you love them with all your heart, you can never go wrong in raising them. And at the end, you children will reciprocate to you all the love and attention you showered to them once they are older. Whatever you give them will be given back to you in time.

Your Free Gift

I wanted to show my appreciation that you support my work so I've put together a free gift for you.

FREE BOOK - Unique Baby Names and Meanings

http://booklife.pro/toddler_bonus

Just visit the link above to download it now.

I know you will love this gift.

Thanks!

Casey Robson

www.ingramcontent.com/pod-product-compliance
Lightning Source LLC
Chambersburg PA
CBHW070234290526
45789CB00004B/1626